APPLE WA
GU

The Complete Tips and Tricks to Master Hidden Features of the New Apple Watch Series 5 and WatchOS 6

TECH

EXPERT

**Copyright © 2019 Tech Expert
All rights reserved.**

It is not legal to reproduce, duplicate, or transmit any part of this document in either electronic means or in printed format. Recording of this publication is strictly

prohibited.

Printed in the United States of America

TABLE OF CONTENTS

INTRODUCTION i

CHAPTER ONE 1

The Apple Watch Series 5 and OS6 .. 1

What are the differences between Apple Watch Series 4 and Apple Watch Series 5? 5

Why are both versions different from other versions? 6

Is it worth it to buy the new Apple Watch series 5 if we currently have the Series 4? 11

How to set up Apple Watch Series 5 and OS6 15

Where to Power On, Wake and Unlock.. 18

How to change the language on Apple Watch Series 5 and Apple Watch OS6.................................... 20

How to Charge Apple Watch Series 5 and OS6 21

How to Adjust Brightness, Text Size and Sounds on Apple Watch Series 5 and OS6 22

CHAPTER TWO 25

Features of Apple Watch Series 5 and OS6 25

    The basic features of the Apple Watch Series 5 include 25

    Price of Apple Watch Series 5 and OS6 27

CHAPTER THREE 29

How to use Siri on Apple Watch Series 5 and OS6 29

   How to reply live notifications 30

   Respond to unread notifications 32

CHAPTER FOUR 33

How to take screenshots on your Apple Watch successfully 33

CHAPTER FIVE 39

Apple Watch Series 5 and OS6 (Health and Fitness) 39

   How to check and monitor your heart rate 42

   Monitoring your fitness 43

   Cycling tracking on Apple OS6 ... 47

CHAPTER SIX 49

Handling your Apple Watch Series 5 and OS6 49

   Restart Apple Watch 49

   Restore and Reset Apple Watch. 51

Update software 53

CHAPTER SEVEN 54

Settings on Apple Watch Series 5 and OS6 54

   Setting Apple Watch 5 and O6 while using VoiceOver 55

   Where to go to Zoom and Bold .. 60

   About Digital Touch 61

   How to send Digital Touch 62

CHAPTER EIGHT 63

Troubleshooting problems with Apple Watch Series 5 and OS6 63

    How to troubleshoot problems 64

CHAPTER NINE 68

Keeping time with Series 5 and O6. 68

    Discover time in other parts of the world 68

    Make use of a stopwatch 70

CHAPTER TEN 71

Maps on Series 5 and OS6 71

    Check out the map 72

Locate your favorite place on the map 72

CHAPTER ELEVEN 74

Music and Photos 74

How to check photos on Series 5 and OS6 75

Control your photo album or storage 76

How to use shutter timer and viewfinder 77

Scroll through music 78

CHAPTER TWELVE 79

Watch Faces on series 5 and OS6 .. 79

- Features of the watch face 80
- Customize your watch face 82

CHAPTER THIRTEEN 84

How to put a wallpaper GIF on Apple Watch 84

- Customize your Apple Watch with a moving background 85

CHAPTER FOURTEEN 89

How to use ECG on Apple watch series 5 and OS6 89

CHAPTER FIFTEEN 92

Calls on Apple Watch Series 5 and Apple OS6 92

CHAPTER SIXTEEN 95

View Mails 95

CHAPTER SEVENTEEN 99

How to buy with Apple Pay 99

   How to use passbook 100

CHAPTER EIGHTEEN 102

Watch control 102

How to control music on Mac ... 102

Controlling Apple TV 104

CHAPTER NINETEEN 107

Apple Stocks 107

Checking stock at a glance 109

How to add stock information into the watch face 110

CHAPTER TWENTY 112

Weather on Apple Watch Series 5 and OS6 112

Keep track of the weather 113

Check out weather on your watch face 114

CHAPTER TWENTY-ONE 117

Apple Watch safety 117

CHAPTER TWENTY-TWO 122

Messaging App 122

CHAPTER TWENTY-THREE 124

Calendars and Reminder 124

CONCLUSION 127

INTRODUCTION

The Apple Watch has been updated again. If last year there was a complete renovation of smart watch design, this year the changes have been more subtle but equally effective, since it comes to assume one of the historical requests made to the device: that the screen is always on. Until now, if we wanted to see the time, notifications or how our training

Progressed, we had to turn the wrist to bring the watch to the face, or touch on the panel. A movement that in many cases could be uncomfortable, but now this has changed. The new Apple Watch Series 5 keeps the screen always on, not resting, thus being more useful. We may be typing on the keyboard, spinning or in a meeting and we will not have to look directly at the watch to track it.

This radical change in the use of the watch has been achieved thanks to the fact that Apple has changed the technology of the panel that is now

Assembling the Watch. The sensations are the same as with the previous generation: same brightness, intensity, fluidity and definition; However, now the panel has been created with an exclusive technology called LTPO (low temperature oxide and polysilicon), which allows the screen to dynamically adjust the refresh rate between 60 Hz to 1 Hz, It allows you to be much more efficient when not in use.

And is that one of the great challenges that Apple had to deal with, having a screen that is on all the

Time but at the same time withstand the whole day. We will not find an improvement over the previous generation, but we can end the day without problems, making the night load still almost mandatory.

The screen reduces its brightness when we are not looking at it and returns to its usual brightness when we turn the wrist or touch it. In the resting position, our sphere will change slightly so that we know that it is at rest, even so, we can see if we receive notifications even if the screen is inactive. Of course, many of

Them will be blurred to preserve the privacy of the message, if we wish.

Even if the screen is always on, if the user wishes, you can deactivate this option and extend the battery life. We will not have a radical saving but it can be useful if we have little load and we have to do a training or place ourselves on a map.

And is that one of the novelties that brings the new Apple Watch Series 5 is the compass. Now the clock is more independent and we can leave the iPhone at home even if we want to use map services or go hiking. This

Tool is not only perfect for those who love trekking and getting lost in the mountains, but also for star lovers. With the Night Sky app you can see on your watch the position of the different constellations.

Now it incorporates both a compass and an elevation meter, so that the user can draw routes and place them more comfortably and accurately. In this book, we are going to show you how to use some hidden features that comes with the new Apple watch series 5

CHAPTER ONE

The Apple Watch Series 5 and OS6

The Apple Watch becomes a luxury watch thanks to titanium

For the first time in its history, the Apple Watch Series 5 has a titanium version, a metal that has always belonged to luxury watchmaking.

This new material brings more lightness to the model and being hypoallergenic, which will allow many people who have so far not been able to wear an Apple Watch to wear it. Another latest development in the Apple Watch Series 5 is the built-in compass. The job of the built-in compass in the Apple Watch Series 5 is that it will show you (wearer) the latitude and longitude, heading, and elevation whenever you make use of your watch for running, hiking, or any other activities done outside the home.

A safety feature to the cellular model of the Apple Watch Series 5 is what makes the latest Apple Watch stand out. The new Apple Watch Series 5 has a free international emergency calling, which means that whenever you hold the crown on Series 5, it will automatically dial the emergency call for that particular country. For example, in the US, the emergency number is 911, so if you hold the crown on the Apple Watch Series 5 for a long time, 911 will automatically dial.

The best thing that can ever happen to any Apple Watch development is the introduction of an App store, and that is what has been made available in the Apple Watch OS6, which differs from other Apple Watches.

This new development is important because it halts any further approach by Apple users to install applications through their iPhone before sending it to their Apple Watches. You can search for your favorite app with your voice by using either Scribble or the popular Siri.

Besides, the Apple Watch 5 will also let you be able to get 2-factor authentication codes directly to your Apple Watch for you to be able to sign in to websites or Platforms with your different Apple devices faster.

What are the differences between Apple Watch Series 4 and Apple Watch Series 5?

With Keynote last September, Apple introduced a new generation of Apple Watch with several improvements over 2018. But, are these improvements sufficient to justify its renewal if we already have an Apple Watch Series 4? Let's see its main novelties.

Why are both versions different from other versions?

Well, as we can see from their new and updated features, the Apple Watch Series 5 and OS6 are very much different from other versions. For the Apple Watch Series 5, the mind-blowing update that came with it is the always-on screen, which will undoubtedly be of help for people that will wear it. Also, this new feature does not bring down the battery's life, and that is why it is more than enticing for Apple lovers. The local emergency calling is also one of the most significant developments that make the Apple Watch Series 5 different from other versions.

The Apple Watch series 5 most noticeable difference from other past versions is the ability to download apps from the App store without needing an iPhone. Other developments that stood out are seen in the features which may include the calculator app, among others.

Screen always on.

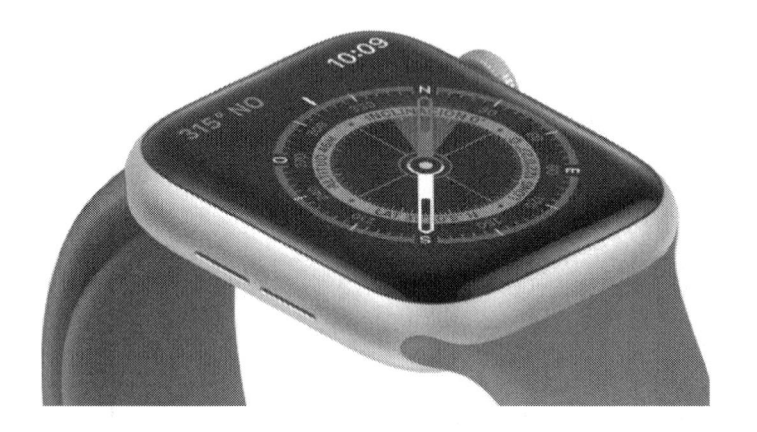

One of the most demanded features by Apple Watch users for the Series 5 was an "Always-on display". Now the Watch will allow us to always see what is on the screen, such as time or information when we are exercising, without having to touch it or perform the typical wrist lift movement. In Series 4 we do not have this feature.

Built-in compass

The new Apple Watch Series 5 now has a built-in compass, as well as a new application for use. With this new function, the clock also offers us information such as the inclination, altitude, latitude and longitude of our location. On the other hand, the main beneficiary of the incorporation of a compass in the Watch is the Maps application, which can now detect our address for example to always have the map towards us and thus facilitate navigation with it. The Apple Watch Series 4 does not have these new features available.

New materials for the Apple Watch Series 5

If you are one of those people who take the Apple watch theme to the next level, then maybe you are interested in this. And Apple has launched this year two new materials that were not available in the previous generation. On the one hand the ceramic has been recovered, which since the 3rd generation was not available and on the other, titanium has been incorporated in two finishes, one light and one dark. Beyond the advantages that these materials offer at the level of resistance over the models for example of aluminum, it is worth noting the fact that the Titanium Watch becomes the lightest of all, surpassing even the aluminum model

Is it worth it to buy the new Apple Watch series 5 if we currently have the Series 4?

The answer in our own opinion varies. If you think you are going to take advantage of the new features, or you want to make an update of your device with new materials, the Apple Watch Series 5 is an option that will not disappoint you. But, on the other hand, if a feature such as the screen is always on is not really transcendental for you or you certainly value the stability of the battery that the Series 4 already has, it may not be worth it.

The compass, a great improvement that triggers its functionality

Apple Watch Series 5 has an integrated compass that will not only serve so that nature lovers don't get lost - that's what Apple Maps is already for. This new piece (yes, it is a hardware additive) will help us to find a restaurant in a simple way - we will simply have to follow the instructions that appear on the screen, in the Yelp app or to locate a constellation in the sky of stars thanks to the Night Sky app. It will be the application developers can use their imagination to take advantage of this new piece.

In addition, the watch also recognizes how high we are and the inclination of the terrain, an information although it can be used so that we enjoy our walks more and also so that the Training application can better measure the efforts we make. How do you achieve it? Well, thanks to the data collected from its integrated barometric altimeter, GPS, Wi-Fi and also data recorded in the Maps app.

How to set up Apple Watch Series 5 and OS6

For you to set up your Apple Watch Series 5 and OS6, there is always a setup assistant that will guide you through some easy steps and also enable you to pair it with your iPhone. There is a screen that will guide you through setting up your Apple Watch.

For you to be able to set up your Apple Watch Series 5 and OS6, you must first update your iPhone to iOS version 8.2. You can locate it by visiting your settings, click on General, and then you will see Software Update, which also has the Apple Watch app. You are then required to click on the Apple Watch app on your iPhone.

The next step for you to take is to wear your Apple Watch on your wrist and then follow the next level by pressing and holding the side button until you can view the Apple logo. When an action comes up, you will then have to place your iPhone in a way to enable the Apple Watch shows in the camera viewfinder on the iPhone screen. You will have to adhere carefully to the instructions on your iPhone and Apple Watch for the setup to be complete. At the time when you are setting up your Apple Watch, there will be a list of language options, and you will have to choose the one you want. Also, during the setup, you will view a Passcode and watch how it will do.

It is important to make sure your Apple Watch is fully charged up to an extent before proceeding to pair it with your iPhone. For your Apple

Watch to work correctly, it has to be fixed perfectly on your wrist.

Where to Power On, Wake and Unlock

A user of the Apple Watch Series 5 and OS6 can power on their watch by pressing and holding the side button until the Apple logo displays. Note that the screen of the Apple Watch might be black for a short period before the Apple logo will show.

Powering off the Apple Watch Series 5 and OS6 is as easy as anything. You will have to press and hold the side button as well until the display of a slider. The slider has to be dragged to the right for the powering off to be complete.

Waking of the Apple Watch Series 5 and OS6 can be done by lifting your wrist or just tapping on the screen of the Apple Watch. Note that the Apple Watch 5 and OS6 will sleep when you lower your wrist. In cases whereby the Apple Watch 5 and OS6 do not wake when you raise your wrist, go to settings, then general and click on orientation, endeavor that the orientation situated on your wrist.

How to change the language on Apple Watch Series 5 and Apple Watch OS6

Language can be changed on the Apple Watch Series 5 and Apple Watch OS6 by opening the Apple Watch on your iPhone, then click on My Watch, go to General, and there you will see Language and Region. Tap on the Language and Region and change it to your preferred one.

How to Charge Apple Watch Series 5 and OS6

You should charge your Apple Watch Series 5 and Watch OS6 in an area where air passes. Position the Apple Watch Magnetic Charging Cable on a smooth surface, then plug it into the power adapter and finally into a power outlet. You can also opt to `connect the power adapter with any apple device such as the iPad and iPhone.

When plugged into a power outlet, the original symbol, which is usually red, will turn green to signify that your Apple Watch is charging.

How to Adjust Brightness, Text Size and Sounds on Apple Watch Series 5 and OS6

For you to adjust your brightness, you will have to open the Settings app. There you will see Brightness when you navigate. Click on the brightness sign for you to either increase or decrease the brightness. In this same part (Settings), you will also see Text size when you also navigate. When you see the Text Size, it is then your decision to either make the text larger, smaller, or medium. Besides, you can as well make the text bold.

For sounds, you will also be required to open the Settings app on your Apple Watch Series 5 and Apple Watch OS6. When the settings app has opened, navigate through until you see Sound and Haptics. Click on the volume buttons, which located underneath the Ringer and Alert sounds, and you will be able to adjust the sound.

There is also an option to mute the sound of your Apple Watch Series 5 and OS6. The need for Muting is for a user not to be disturbed by any sound. You mustn't forget to adjust the sound from mute when you finish with what you are doing that does not demand noise or unnecessary notification.

CHAPTER TWO
Features of Apple Watch Series 5 and OS6

The basic features of the Apple Watch Series 5 include:

1. Tracking of one's fitness
2. Siri commands
3. Time telling
4. Turn-by-turn navigation
5. ECG monitoring
6. Workout tracking

7. Receiving messages and notifications

8. Monitor heart rate

9. Updated map app and built-in compass

10. 18-hour battery life capacity

11. Always-on display

12. Much better refresh rates and low-power display driver

The features of the Apple Watch OS6 include:

1. Watch Independent Apps

2. Audiobooks app

3. New calculator app

4. Updates on health and activity

5. Automatic software updates

6. Developed timekeeping

7. Shazam integration (Siri)

Price of Apple Watch Series 5 and OS6

Due to its usefulness and durability, the Apple Watch Series 5 sells for $399 for a model known as the GPS model. There is also another type of Apple Watch Series 5, which is known as the cellular model, which costs in the region of $499.

On the other hand, the Apple Watch OS6 goes for a similar price, though the two Apple Watches were both released around the same time.

CHAPTER THREE
How to use Siri on Apple Watch Series 5 and OS6

With the help of Siri on your Apple Watch, certain functions or information can be passed on.

Siri does the primary function of answering the questions you might have in mind and which you will utter. To ask Siri a question, you will have to make sure your screen is awake on the Apple Watch. The next step for you to take is to say, Hey Siri," after which you will utter whatever you want to say.

Another way you can ask Siri a question is by clicking and holding the Digital Crown till you can view the listening indicator, which lies below the screen, then you can proceed to say your question and release the Digital Crown immediately you are done asking your query to Siri. For you to reply to Siri, you will also have to follow the same steps above.

How to reply live notifications

While using your Apple Watch Series 5 or Apple Watch OS6, and notification just popped into your Apple Watch, tap on the screen to then view it. In some cases, the notification may appear directly to your screen, and so it is left for you to view it immediately or later on.

You can as well dismiss or close any notification that comes into your Apple Watch by navigating to the bottom of the notification and click dismiss.

Respond to unread notifications

In some instances, you might be so busy that you will not be able to read a particular message or view a specific notification that comes into your Apple Watch. You can always go back and read your unread notifications because it automatically saves in the notification center. When a red dot at the top of your Apple Watch begins to show, it means you have an unread notification. You can then navigate downwards to view your unread notifications and reply to them.

CHAPTER FOUR

How to take screenshots on your Apple Watch successfully

The screenshots on the Apple Watch can be done, but you have to follow a few different steps from the iPhone.

Here we explain how to do it and how and where to see the photos.

Taking screenshots on the Apple Watch is possible. Perhaps you have not seen the need to do it yet as with your mobile, or perhaps you have tried a thousand times to make a capture but you have ended up blocking and unlocking the clock hundreds of times. It happens to the best, don't worry.

The truth is that doing so is very easy, especially if you have had practice with any of the pre-X iPhone, but if you are new to Apple or have not yet got used to the smartwatch, there is no problem because we have found the steps to continue to take a screenshot on the Apple Watch successfully, and as we said it is very easy, as long as you have activated this function, of course. And is that unlike the iPhone, in the Apple watch we must activate the screenshots in the settings to be able to do them.

Here are the steps to follow:

A, Go to Settings - general - activate screenshots.

B, Press the side button and the digital crown at the same time for a few seconds (it may take practice).

C, Ready, the screen will go blank for a second, which will indicate that the capture has been made just like the iPhone. Also if you have it in sound you will hear the typical camera noise.

And how can you see the photos? As it says in the settings section, the photos are automatically saved in the photo album but from the iPhone, not from the Apple Watch. If you want to access them through your mobile, you will have to go to the album, go to the "content types" section and access the screenshots there.

But if we want to have these images on our smart watch, we will have to do a little more. For this it is necessary to synchronize an album of your mobile with the smartwatch by following these steps:

A, Access the iPhone Watch app.

B, Go to the photos section - synchronized albums.

C, Choose the album we want to synchronize (recent, favorites, a created specifically for this ...)

From now on you can make the captures you want and see them on the device you prefer. Maybe pressing the two buttons on the clock at the same time does not come out perfect at first, But with a little practice you will get it better.

CHAPTER FIVE

Apple Watch Series 5 and OS6 (Health and Fitness)

The Apple Watch Series 5 and OS6 have been designed to track your health and fitness and also to watch over how your body runs throughout a particular day and beyond.

How to track daily activity

The job of the Activity app on your Apple Watch Series 5 and OS6 is to keep track of how to move throughout the day and also tries its possible best to make your reach your fitness goals. With the help of the activity app, you will track how many times you move, how frequent you stand on your feet, and how to be able to keep up with the day's work.

To be able to track your daily activity on the Apple Watch Series 5 and OS6, you will first have to open the Activity app and the move towards the left so that you can read the moving exercise and stand descriptions and select Get Started. You will have to fill some necessary information, which may include Age, Sex, Weight, and

Height. When you finish, click on, continue, and begin your movement.

As an Apple Watch user who uses the activity app on a regular or daily basis, you can as well track your movement by opening the activity glance. Navigate till you also find the individual activities, and you can even view how many calories you have already burned. Before the commencement of your daily activity, you will have to set your goal. Whenever an overlapping ring comes up, it means you have exceeded your target, and you can adjust it also.

How to check and monitor your heart rate

To obtain the best results from the Apple Watch Series 5 and Os6 as regards checking and monitoring your heart rate, the back of your Apple Watch must require skin contact for you to get the features of skin detection, heart rate sensor, and haptic notification.

Checking your heart rate requires you to wear your Apple Watch the right way, not too tight to the wrist, and not also lose. Whenever you are doing your fitness workouts, your Apple

Watch needs to be tight to your wrist so that it might not fall off.

For you to see your present heart rate, you will be required to navigate to the top of your Apple Watch and select the Heartbeat glance to monitor your heart rate and check out what your heart reads.

Monitoring your fitness

There is a workout app on your Apple Watch Series 5 and OS6 that enables you to be able to track your fitness and also manage your fitness sessions. With the help of the workout app, you can set your desired goals and objectives, which may include calories to burn, time, and distance.

You can begin your fitness by clicking on workout and doing the one you wish. The goal screen enables you to be able to select your calorie, distance, or time. It is also important to note that outdoor and indoor walk or workouts are quite different from each other, and the Apple Watch Series 5 and Apple Watch Series OS6 calculates them differently. While working out inside your home, you might not need the services of your iPhone, like when you will be working out outside the comfort of your home.

You can also monitor the progress of your fitness by viewing the completion ring. You will be able to see if your time has gone by, your average and fastest pace, the calories you may have burned, and the distance you may have covered as well.

Also, you can pause and resume your workouts anytime you want, and this is done by pressing the display and clicking on pause, and the same thing applies whenever you want to continue your exercise.

Whenever you want to work out for a long time, and you do not want your battery to be diminishing, you can opt for the option of disabling the heartbeat sensor on your Apple Watch Series 5 and Apple Watch OS6. However, the number of calories you may have burned may not be so accurate due to this.

At the sound of an alarm on your Apple Watch Series 5 and OS6, it means that you have achieved your goal, and you can go ahead to end it and continue later on when you must have gained full strength. You also review your fitness and your recent workout but with the help of an iPhone. Select the date you want to view on the activity app, and then you will see the summaries of that day.

Cycling tracking on Apple OS6

It is important to be aware that the cycling app on Apple Os6 is not for cyclists; instead, it is specifically for women. Female health has been made easy with the introduction of the Apple Watch OS6 with features that include symptoms, cycle length, variations, and logging of flow level.

Through this data, the cycle tracking app will let you know when it guesses that your next call of action is about to begin. Also, the whole thing is synced back to your iPhone through the Health app.

CHAPTER SIX
Handling your Apple Watch Series 5 and OS6

This part of this book will show you the best ways on how to manage your Apple Watch Series 5 and Apple Watch OS6, so let's get into it.

Restart Apple Watch

Restarting your Apple Watch is important in a case whereby something or an app is acting up.

You can restart your Apple Watch by selecting and holding the side button until you see a slider, move the power off slider to the right of your screen for your Apple Watch to go off. Then go ahead and press the side button again and wait until the Apple logo comes back on for you to turn your Apple Watch back on.

There is also something we refer to as force Apple Watch restart. You should do it when Apple Watch fails to restart the proper way. For the force Apple Watch to restart, you will have to press the side button down and also the Digital Crown simultaneously for about ten seconds, until you can see the Apple logo.

Restore and Reset Apple Watch

In an unfortunate case whereby your Apple Watch is disabled, or you might have forgotten your passcode, you can make adequate use of the Apple Watch app on your iPhone to enable you to enter the passcode once again. Meanwhile, for some people who still cannot remember their passcode, restoring and resetting the passcode is the only option left. Whenever you want to restore, remember that you will be clearing the content and settings on your Apple Watch.

For you to reset the Apple Watch, you will have to open the settings app and then click on general, and then an option for a reset will come up. When it comes up, click on erase all content and settings.

When the reset has finished, your Apple Watch will then have to restart, and you will be required to pair your Apple Watch with an iPhone again.

Update software

Whenever there is a new update, you should follow the trend of updating your software in the Apple Watch on your iPhone.

You can check for new updated software by opening the Apple Watch on your iPhone and click on My Watch. The next step for you to take is to visit the general and then software update. What you will have to do if there is a new software is to download the software to your iPhone and then to your Apple Watch.

CHAPTER SEVEN

Settings on Apple Watch Series 5 and OS6

The option settings is a very important section in every device because it depicts and helps you to change some specific things you do not want anymore. Exploring settings on your Apple Watch Series 5 and OS6 will enable you to see things that will amaze you.

Setting Apple Watch 5 and O6 while using VoiceOver

The major use of the VoiceOver is to make your Apple Watch effective even if you cannot view the screen of your Apple Watch. Here, we are going to learn how to set up Apple Watch Series 5 and OS6 while using VoiceOver.

The basic steps needed for setting up Apple Watch while using VoiceOver includes;

- Switch the Apple Watch to display mode.

- Switch on the VoiceOver by pressing the Digital Crown on three occasions.

- Go left or right on display to select a language and click on it twice to select it.

- Move right of the display to highlight the Start pairing button and also click on it twice.

- Turn on VoiceOver on your iPhone

- Open the Apple Watch app by going to the iPhone home screen and moving right to choose the

Apple Watch app and click on it twice.

• When iPhone wants to pair, move right and click on the Start Pairing button and then click on it twice. Hold your Apple watch at the top of the camera screen shows.

• You can pair automatically by showing the iPhone camera at the watch from around 6 inches.

• Move right for you to choose the pair Apple Watch with your hand and click on it twice.

• With your Apple Watch, you can go ahead to find the Apple Watch ID.

- With the possession of an iPhone, choose your Apple Watch and move right until you are sure you heard the Apple Watch identifier that will show and then click twice.

- To obtain your pairing code, move right, and a six-digit code will be said.

- Put in the pairing code from your Apple Watch to your iPhone via the keypad. When successful, you will also hear that Apple has been "paired."

- After pairing has completed, move to the right on your iPhone for you to set up the Apple Watch button and also click twice.

- Review the terms and conditions and agree to them.

- You can put in your password for the Apple identification by moving right to the enter password button and enter your Apple ID you made use of on your iPhone.

- You can select a location by moving to your favorite one and clicking twice.

- You can select a Siri option by moving to your favorite one and also clicking twice.

- You can also create an Apple Watch passcode. The basic thing here to do is to move right on the passcode to choose to Create a passcode and then double-tap. With your Apple Watch, put in a four-digit passcode you like and then put it again to confirm. Move your finger around the screen to choose a number and click twice.

• With your Apple Watch, select if you want to unlock Apple Watch when you unlock your iPhone or not.

• You can also choose to install additional apps on your Apple Watch.

Where to go to Zoom and Bold

You can zoom on your Apple Watch Series 5 and OS6 by opening the

Settings app and then turn to general and accessibility, and there you will find zoom. The same thing will apply when you also want to bold your text on your Apple Watch Series 5 and OS6.

About Digital Touch

The Digital Touch on your Apple watch enables you to send sketches or even your heartbeat to anybody. You can open the digital touch by clicking on the side button of your Apple Watch to view your friends and select on a friend and tap on the

Digital Touch button at the bottom of the photo. However, you will only be able to view the Digital Touch icon if your friend owns an Apple Watch.

How to send Digital Touch

You can send a digital touch by sending a sketch or your heartbeat. There is an image, the left side will show what is sent, and the image on the right shows the notifications that you have seen.

CHAPTER EIGHT

Troubleshooting problems with Apple Watch Series 5 and OS6

The major problems users of Apple Watch Series 5 and OS6 encounter daily is the problem of battery life. Now, Apple, while releasing both watches, clearly stated that they have an 18-hour battery life, but the users of both Apple Watches do not agree to this fact. They often complain that the battery dies quickly, and they do not get up to that 18-hour they had earlier hoped to get.

The problem here is that most Apple Watch users make use of their Apple Watch more than required, and that is why the battery does not last any longer for them. Whenever you are not using a particular app on your Apple Watch, you should close them for your battery not to waste unnecessarily.

How to troubleshoot problems

If you are an Apple Watch user who is undergoing several issues with your

Apple Watch and you are not enjoying the way your watch you spent good money on is acting up, then you should endeavor to seek an immediate solution.

Troubleshooting problems may be in the form of your Apple Watch not being able to power on, not also been able to text or receive messages, battery problems, not able to make calls and so on, you can visit any Apple outlet to fix these problems or their official site to ask questions on how to fix the problems. Apple also has a support forum in which you can join and get in contact if you want to solve the problems you are encountering with your Apple Watch.

Below, we will take a look at some problems associated with Apple Watch and how to solve them. They include:

Problems – Battery issue

Solutions – Turn off the Always-on Display screen and stop all apps currently not in use.

Problems – Problems connecting to the cellular

Solution – You will have to update your Apple Watch software if the problem persists, try setting up your cellular plan once again.

Problems–Digital crown not working

Solutions – Clean the watch thoroughly or visit the Apple official guide if the problem continues.

These are just a few of the problems and how to solve them, which are associated with the Apple Watch Series 5 and Apple Watch OS6.

CHAPTER NINE
Keeping time with Series 5 and O6

Having the feature of time in the Apple Watch Series 5 and OS6, you will be able to view the time in other countries of the world and as well use timers and set alarms.

Discover time in other parts of the world

There is a World Clop app on your Apple Watch Series 5 and OS6, which allows you to view the time in countries and cities of the world. Just open the app, and you will be amazed. To see time in other cities of the world, open the World Clock app, move to the city you want to view their time, and there you have it.

Set your alarm

The alarm plays a significant role in the life of anyone that wants to keep the time of something. Open the Alarm clock and tap on it to set your alarm to whatever you want it to be.

How to use a timer

Timer app on your Apple Watch Series 5 and Watch OS6 lets you keep up of time. Open the timer app, choose whether you want it at hours or minutes, and click on start.

Make use of a stopwatch

The stopwatch is an app on the Apple Watch Series 5 and OS6, open the app, and click on start to begin. When you finish, there is a stop button there to end it.

CHAPTER TEN
Maps on Series 5 and OS6

You can view the map on your Apple Watch Series 5 and OS6 when you open the map app. In the map app, you can see a location. Searching for a location on the map app is quite easy, click on search and begin to look for your desired location. With the map app, you can even get information as regards your stated landmark.

Check out the map

It is much easier to check out the map app on your Apple Watch Series 5 and OS6. Just open your display screen and look for the map app. Open it and begin to explore the world at your fingertips.

Locate your favorite place on the map

In order to locate your favorite places on the map app on your Apple

Watch, click on destination landmark after you must have opened the map app and then keep moving until you view directions, then click on walking or driving depending on what you are currently doing and then you are on your way to locating your favorite place on the map.

When you finally locate your favorite place on the map, you can then get directions to that particular place from where you are currently staying.

CHAPTER ELEVEN
Music and Photos

The music app is one of the most important apps for an individual, and that is why it is much needed on the Apple Watch Series 5 and OS6 by its users. Open the music app on your Apple Watch, go through your songs, playlists, artists, album or songs and play any of them you want. You can also explore with the music app by creating your collection, repeating songs or reshuffling them.

There is an iPhone album in your Apple Watch that enables you to view your photos. What you will have to do is to open the photo app on your Apple Watch and begin to scroll through your favorite images. Delete and edit your favorite pictures with the photo app if you want.

How to check photos on Series 5 and OS6

You can check your photos on your Apple Watch Series 5 and OS6 by opening the Photo app. The photo app is on your Apple Watch, open it and check your album for you to begin to see your photos and bring back memories.

Control your photo album or storage

You need to know that the Apple Watch store images from a single synced photo album with your iPhone.

You can create a new photo album by visiting and using the photo app. controlling the storage capacity on your Apple Watch is very important, especially if you still wish to store other things on your Apple Watch. To save storage, you can limit the photo storage to whatever you want. Open the Apple Watch app on your iPhone, and then click on my watch and go to photos, there you will see the photo limit option.

How to use shutter timer and viewfinder

The shutter timer on your Apple Watch is for the sole purpose of a group shot. To access the shutter timer, you will first have to open the camera app and then click on the timer button located at the lower right. The next thing that happens is that a tap, beep, and flashes from your iPhone will show that you should be expecting the shot soon.

What the timer does is to take plenty of shots, select the good ones out of the list and delete the ones you do not want.

Scroll through music

It is quite easy with the help of the music app on your Apple Watch Series 5 and OS6. Open the music app; check out your playlist, songs, albums, and artists.

CHAPTER TWELVE

Watch Faces on series 5 and OS6

Watch face is one of the features you can find on the Apple Watch Series 5 and Apple Watch OS6. In the watch face app, there are designs, colors, and other features that are very much capable of blowing your mind off.

Features of the watch face

The Apple Watch has a lot of features that we will be taking a look at below. They include:

1. Astronomy – What the feature, Astronomy, does is to allow you to see the solar system and the exact position where the planets, sun, and moon are.

2. Chronograph–The job of the Chronograph as a feature of the watch face is to measure time in an exact increase — for example, a classic analog stopwatch.

3. Color–This feature does the job of showing the time.

4. Mickey Mouse – This feature is designed to show you a different view of time via the Mickey mouse design

5. Modular – This feature has a gird design, which allows one to include as many functions in one screen to guide you throughout the day.

6. Simple – The=is feature allows you to include detail to the dial and also corners.

7. Motion – This feature is known to be a very beautiful one, as it shows incredible animated themes that may include butterflies or flowers.

8. X-large – Allows you to see time and day on a large face.

9. Solar– This feature of the watch face is also magnificent. Your present location and time of the day will show the sun's position in the sky and even the day, time, and date.

Customize your watch face

The watch face also enables you to flex and change it to the way you wish so that it can suit your style. In the customization, you can select from a list of watch face designs, features, and colors and include it to your collection.

When the watch face is showing, you can click on display and move to view the faces in your collection. At the point when you see the watch face you need, select it.

CHAPTER THIRTEEN

How to put a wallpaper GIF on Apple Watch

The Apple Watch is one of the Apple devices that we can customize the most thanks to a wide variety of spheres and complications, those small mini apps that we can put in different areas of the watch. But what many Apple watch users don't know is that you can also use a GIF as an animated wallpaper on the Apple Watch.

Doing it is easier than it seems and we will explain how to get it step by step, as it usually happens, it is a process that you have to perform on your iPhone.

Customize your Apple Watch with a moving background

The first thing you should know is that Apple does not allow you to put GIFs directly as an animated wallpaper on your Apple Watch, but it does allow you to do so with Live Photos.

Fortunately, the largest GIF application in the App Store allows us to download any GIF in Live Photo format. So the first step is to download Giphy

Once you have downloaded the app, enter and search for your favorite GIF.

When you click on download remember to do it as Live Photo.

Now go to the Photos app, find the GIF you just downloaded, open it and click on Edit.

Click on the Live Photo icon, slide your finger down to the right and click on Convert to a key photo, so that will be the last image to be displayed and it will look better.

Now save the edition by clicking on Ok.

Click on the share button below on the left and look for Create sphere.

Now select Sphere Photos and you can edit some settings of the dial, such as the position of the watch.

Once you have everything ready click on Add.

On your Apple Watch you just have to slide sideways until you find your new dial.

Now every time you look at the time you will see a small animation of the GIF you downloaded and the sphere of your Apple Watch will be much more fun than before. You have millions of options and you can create all the spheres you want, just keep in mind that the duration should not be too long, if you have any problem try reducing the duration of the Live Photo from the photos app settings.

CHAPTER FOURTEEN
How to use ECG on Apple watch series 5 and OS6

Open the ECG on your Apple Watch Series 5 and OS6; then, for you to get accurate results, you will need to place your arms in your lap or a desk and leave a finer on the digital crown for as long as you are counting. Make sure you stay still because if you move, the test will no longer be as accurate as you expect it.

Also, endeavor that the Apple Watch is glued to your wrist. A 30-second test will be conducted, and when completed, you will receive one of three results, which include atrial fibrillation (aFib), which means your heart is beating irregularly. The second result is Sinus rhythm, which means that your heart is beating uniformly. The last of the results are inconclusive, which means that the app did not read your heart well.

Ways to interpret ECG

You can interpret the ECG when you open the app on your Apple Watch. The ECG app is a white circle with a red line kind of color, which looks somehow related to a heart rate reading.

CHAPTER FIFTEEN

Calls on Apple Watch Series 5 and Apple OS6

Phone calls are a very integral part of any device, whether phone or watch. The Apple Watch Series 5 and Apple Watch OS6 is in no exception as regards the phone app. The phone app allows you to make calls to your loved ones and pass necessary information whenever you cannot physically see them.

How to answer phone calls

Answering a call on your Apple Watch Series 5 or OS6 may look tricky to a lot of people. Whenever there is an incoming call on your Apple Watch, you will have to raise your wrist for you to wake up your Apple Watch and view the person calling you. Then you will have to tap on the answer button for you to talk while using the microphone and speaker located on the Apple Watch. The above way is just the simple method on how to answer phone calls on the Apple Watch Series 5 and OS6.

How to make phone calls from Apple watch series 5 and OS6 to iPhone

Placing a call on the Apple Watch Series 5 and watch OS6 is as easy as answering a call. What you will have to do is to open the phone app and then click on contacts, type in, or scroll to the name you wish to call and then place your call.

CHAPTER SIXTEEN
View Mails

The mail is a form of official communication between 2 people or an individual and a company. A lot of people often make use of it, including users of the Apple Watch.

How to check out your emails on Apple watch series 5 and Apple watch OS6

There is no other way for you to check out your mail on your Apple Watch Series 5 and OS6 without the use of the Mail app. Open the Mail app and then turn the digital crown to move through the message list and click on a message that catches your interest. You can also read your mail through the notification if you intentionally set it in that direction.

Managing your mails

It is very necessary and right for you to know how to be able to manage your mails on your Apple Watch. Managing your mails requires you to flag your mail messages. When you read a message in your Mail, click on display and then select the flag. Flagging of a message can also be done when you preview it in a notification.

You can also manage your emails by changing the flag style. The flag style can be changed if you open the Apple Watch app on your iPhone and go to mail, then the custom, there you will see the flag style.

Managing your mail also requires you to be able to mark a mail as read or unread even after you must have read it. Also, deleting a particular mail message is one of the ways through which you are managing your emails. If you view a mail message and you do not like the content, or you feel it is a spam message, you can choose to delete it by opening the mail app and clicking on trash. As a user of the Apple Watch Series 5 and OS6, you can also select the kind of mailbox which will appear on your Apple Watch, and this is done with the help of an iPhone.

CHAPTER SEVENTEEN

How to buy with Apple Pay

The Apple Watch is designed to use Apple Pay to buy in stores that accept only payments without contact. What you will have to do is to set up Apple Pay on your Apple Watch app on your iPhone, and you will begin to buy.

Note that if you go ahead to unpair Apple Watch and disable your passcode, you will not be able to use Apple Pay.

The eight (8) credits will show at the top of the stack in your passbook app. Meanwhile, the last four (4) digits of your credit or debit card number will also show on the payment card. US credit and debit cards can be used with Apple Pay easily.

How to use passbook

The purpose of the passbook app on your Apple Watch is to keep your boarding passes, loyalty cards, and movie tickets. Your passbook on your iPhone will automatically sync to the Apple Watch. You will have to scan a pass on the Apple Watch for you to view and check-in for a flight, redeem a coupon, and check-in for a movie.

You can also check for options for your passes on your Apple Watch by opening the Apple Watch on your iPhone, click on My Watch, and tap on Passbook and Apple Pay.

CHAPTER EIGHTEEN
Watch control

It is essential to get full control over your Apple Watch Series 5 and OS6, and this will give you authority over all the apps on your Apple Watch. Let us then start with how to control music on Mac via the Apple Watch.

How to control music on Mac

With the help of the Remote app on your Apple Watch Series 5 and Watch

OS6, you can play music on iTunes on a Mac with the same Wi-Fi network.

The Remote app does everything as regards controlling music on your Mac via the Apple Watch. You can also add an iTunes library by opening your Apple Watch and clicking on Add Device +. Other things you can do is to choose a library to play from, remove the library, and also control playback options on the remote app, which can be seen in the Apple Watch.

Controlling Apple TV

Controlling the Apple TV is also a significant point in the life of your Apple Watch Series 5 and OS6. As an Apple Watch user, you can control your Apple TV by making use of the remote control on your Apple Watch whenever you join the same Wi-Fi network.

Furthermore, you can also pair your Apple Watch with your Apple TV. Pairing your Apple Watch with your Apple TV can be done by firstly joining the Wi-Fi network that Apple TV is connected to.

Open the remote app on your Apple Watch and click on Add device. When you then turn on your Apple TV, visit settings and go to general and remotes and choose your Apple Watch and go-ahead to enter the passcode, which will show on your Apple Watch. Whenever a pairing icon shows close to the Apple Watch, then the Apple Watch will be able to control the Apple TV.

For your Apple Watch to control an Apple TV, endeavor that your Apple TV is awake and then open the remote app on your Apple Watch. Select on Apple TV and then navigate around the Apple TV menu list and choose on the items. After completion, you have successfully been able to control the Apple TV with your Apple Watch Series 5 and OS6.

CHAPTER NINETEEN
Apple Stocks

The job of the stock app on your Apple Watch Series 5 and OS6 is for you to be able to view certain information on the stocks which you follow with your iPhone.

How to track stocks on Apple watch series 5 and OS6

Tracking your stocks on your Apple Watch is very important so that you do not get to miss any information at all. You can follow the market stock by opening the stocks app on your

Apple Watch. As an Apple Watch user, you can view details about your Apple stock when you click on it in the list and then turn the digital crown to move.

Select the performance graph for the time indicators to show and for you to alter it.

The Apple Watch user can also add a record or delete stocks by making use of the stocks app on your iPhone. Whenever you make a change on the stocks app on your iPhone, it will reflect on your Apple Watch.

Checking stock at a glance

An Apple Watch Series 5 and OS6 user can make adequate use of the stock glance to check your stock of where you have an interest. However, you will initially have to view the stocks glance by scrolling up on the watch face and then scrolling to the stock information.

Select your stock by opening the Apple Watch on your iPhone and click on my Watch, select stocks, and make your decision on the type of stock you want.

How to add stock information into the watch face

Stock information can be added or included in the below watch faces:

1. Mickey Mouse
2. Modular
3. Utility

For you to add information to your stock face, the first step for you to take is to select the display and then click customize. Scroll left till you can see the feature of choosing an individual face. Select your preferred one you wish to make use of and then turn the digital crown to select stocks. After you may have completed the steps mentioned above, you will then have to press the digital crown. You can also select the stock which will be shown on the watch face and as well choose the data you will prefer viewing on the watch face.

CHAPTER TWENTY

Weather on Apple Watch Series 5 and OS6

Knowing the nature of weather of a particular day is very necessary for you to avoid any unfortunate circumstances which may arise like heavy rain, landslide or any other bad weather options. Every one of the Apple Watch users makes adequate use of the weather app on their Apple Watches, and why not you too?

Keep track of the weather

Like what was stated earlier, keeping track of the weather is very much necessary to avoid any bad thing which may arise from the conditions of the weather. You can keep track of the weather by checking the current temperature or current condition of weather when you check the weather glance on your Apple Watch Series 5 and OS6.

Moreover, you can also check weather forecasts and also check out more details when you open the weather app on your Apple Watch and select the city. You can check out weather forecasts in your preferred cities and know the likely weather condition there in a few days.

Check out weather on your watch face

Addition of weather information on these listed watch faces are;

1. Simple

2. Temperature

3. Chronograph

4. Modular

5.   Mickey Mouse

6.   Utility

You can add weather to your watch face on your Apple Watch by clicking on display and then select customize. Move to the left where you will find individual face features and then select the weather information and turn to the digital crown to select the weather. Round up by holding the digital crown. Selecting a city for the watch face weather and opening the full weather app is not also left out.

However, do this when you open the Apple Watch app on your iPhone and click on my watch and visit the weather and default city. For the second part, what you have to do is to click on the temperature on your watch face.

CHAPTER TWENTY-ONE
Apple Watch safety

Safety information is very advisable for you to learn whenever you want to operate any device, including the Apple Watch. The Apple Watch Series 5 and OS6 is made up of different materials which include:

Stainless steel, sapphire crystal, 7000 series aluminum, Ion-X glass, plastic, ceramic, and so on.

The safety information you will need to be wary of when you begin to use the Apple Watch regards the repairing, battery, charging, and distraction, exposure to heat, loss of hearing, skin sensitivities, and many others.

Never attempt to repair the Apple Watch's battery by yourself, or you risk your Apple Watch spoiling further than expected. Make sure you look for the help or assistance of an expert, probably an Apple Watch repairer, to repair the Apple Watch for you.

In the case of the battery, do not make the mistake of removing the battery and fixing it back. While doing so, you may spoil any important thing around the Apple

Watch, and it will cost you a lot of money for you to be able to repair it again.

For distraction, endeavor not to be pressing your Apple Watch while walking on the road to avoid any form of an accident that may likely occur. Also, try not to expose the Apple Watch to heat (hot sun). The Apple Watch may begin to act funny when it is being exposed to heat.

For those set of people who experiences skin reactions whenever they put on jewelry watches or anything of the sort on their wrist, they should wear the Apple Watch only when necessary for the nature of the Apple Watch not to tamper with their skin too much.

There are other varieties of safety information which you will need to take into notice, and you can do that by visiting the Apple Watch guidelines.

Info on band care

You must make use of only Apple bands for you not to tamper with your Apple Watch.

You can clean the band by firstly removing it from the Apple Watch before you begin to clean. Cleaning can be done with a nonabrasive lint-free cloth and always dry it thoroughly. Also, you can change and fasten bands in your Apple Watch.

CHAPTER TWENTY-TWO
Messaging App

How to check out and reply messages

As an Apple Watch user, you can read and reply to messages on your Apple Watch Series 5 and OS6 through the help of your messaging app. Open your message app on your Apple Watch and begin to read and reply to messages. With the messaging app on your Apple Watch Series 5 and OS6, you can also save a photo, view video, listen to an audio clip, and so on.

CHAPTER TWENTY-THREE
Calendars and Reminder

With the help of the calendar app on your Apple Watch Series 5 and OS6, you can check out the current date, future date, and so set reminders for special events. The calendar app can be opened from your Apple Watch. The reminders are also important to enable you to remember certain events that may likely skip your mind.

How to check and update your calendars

You can check the calendar app on your Apple Watch by locating Calendar on your Apple Watch and opening it. When we talk about updating the calendar app, we are referring to adjusting the settings. You can do this when you open the Apple Watch app on your iPhone, select my watch, and then click on the calendar to be able to adjust the settings.

How to set reminders

You can only set a reminder on your iPhone with the help of the Apple Watch app. Since there is no option for a reminder on your Apple Watch, the setting of a reminder can be done by opening the Apple Watch app on your iPhone by making use of Siri and then tell Siri to remind you of a particular event.

CONCLUSION

Apple Watch Series 5 is the most sophisticated and successful version of all Apple Watch that Apple has created. The screen always on is a major advance for the range, especially since it does not involve extra energy expenditure: the battery lasts perfectly one day of intense use.

Its other breakthrough, the inclusion of the compass, is a tool of great value for developers, who can use it to improve the experience in augmented reality video games, to guide us to our destinations or simply to improve our experience practicing cycling or hiking.

The titanium and ceramic editions, in addition to the collaboration with Hermès, bring a touch of luxury to the model. The most notable is undoubtedly the ceramic, a pure white and scratch resistant that will become a status symbol.

All these features add to all the good things that Apple has been providing in recent years to its watch (electrocardiogram, fall sensor, training app, activity rings, the possibility of installing a sim card and make it independent of the iPhone...) to confirm that the Apple Watch remains the absolute reference in the smart watch market.

What room for improvement is left? When Apple decides to install a 5G modem inside, its possibilities will skyrocket. Until then, the Apple Watch Series 5 is the closest to the ideal watch they have in Cupertino.

TECH EXPERT

Printed in Great Britain
by Amazon